W9-BEV-287

★ ★

FLORIDA

by Jonatha A. Brown

GARETH**STEVENS**
PUBLISHING
A Member of the WRC Media Family of Companies

Please visit our web site at: www.garethstevens.com
For a free color catalog describing Gareth Stevens Publishing's
list of high-quality books and multimedia programs, call
1-800-542-2595 (USA) or 1-800-387-3178 (Canada).
Gareth Stevens Publishing's fax: (414) 332-3567.

Library of Congress Cataloging-in-Publication Data

Brown, Jonatha A.
    Florida / Jonatha A. Brown.
      p. cm. — (Portraits of the states)
    Includes bibliographical references and index.
    ISBN 0-8368-4622-2 (lib. bdg.)
    ISBN 0-8368-4641-9 (softcover)
    1. Florida—Juvenile literature. I. Title. II. Series.
   F311.3.B76   2005
   975.9—dc22   2005042615

This edition first published in 2006 by
Gareth Stevens Publishing
A Member of the WRC Media Family of Companies
330 West Olive Street, Suite 100
Milwaukee, WI 53212 USA

This edition copyright © 2006 by Gareth Stevens, Inc.

Editorial direction: Mark J. Sachner
Project manager: Jonatha A. Brown
Editor: Betsy Rasmussen
Art direction and design: Tammy West
Picture research: Diane Laska-Swanke
Indexer: Walter Kronenberg
Production: Jessica Morris and Robert Kraus

Picture credits: Cover, pp. 17, 20, 21, 26, 27 © Corel; p. 4 © Yale Joel/Time &
Life Pictures/Getty Images; pp. 5, 24 Tallahassee Area Conventions and Visitors
Bureau; p. 6 © The Newberry Library/Stock Montage, Inc; p. 7 © Hulton
Archive/Getty Images; p. 11 © Santi Visalli Inc./Getty Images; p. 12 NASA; p. 15
© Fox Photos/Getty Images; p. 22 Gregg Andersen; p. 25 © Tim Sloan/AFP/Getty
Images; p. 28 © Doug Pensinger/Getty Images; p. 29 © Graeme Teague

Printed in the United States of America

1 2 3 4 5 6 7 8 9 09 08 07 06 05

CONTENTS

Words that are defined in the Glossary appear
in **bold** the first time they are used in the text.

On the Cover: The southern part of Florida is known for its warm and
sunny weather. Palm trees are common in this part of the state.

Introduction

If you could visit Florida, where would you go? Walt Disney World? The Kennedy Space Center? A sandy beach? Florida has so many great places to visit.

Florida has a warm climate. It is perfect for plants and animals that cannot live in colder places. Flowers bloom year-round in Florida. Even its name means "flowery" in Spanish.

Many people live in Florida. It has the fourth-largest population of the fifty U.S. states.

Welcome to Orlando! Workers at Walt Disney World pose for a group photo.

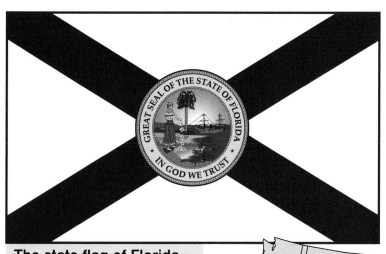

The state flag of Florida.

FLORIDA FACTS

- Became the 27th State: March 3, 1845
- Population (2004): 17,397,161
- Capital: Tallahassee
- Biggest Cities: Jacksonville, Miami, Tampa, St. Petersburg
- Size: 53,927 square miles (139,671 square kilometers)
- Nickname: The Sunshine State
- State Tree: Sabal palmetto palm
- State Flower: Orange blossom
- State Animal: Florida panther
- State Bird: Mockingbird

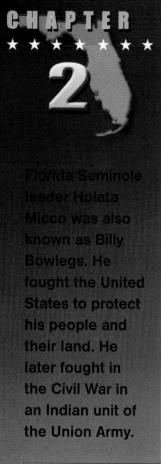

Florida Seminole leader Holata Micco was also known as Billy Bowlegs. He fought the United States to protect his people and their land. He later fought in the Civil War in an Indian unit of the Union Army.

History

Native Americans have lived in Florida for thousands of years. The first people came from the north and west. They hunted animals and caught shellfish. They found plants and nuts to eat.

Later, they planted beans, squash, and corn. Their crops grew well in the warm climate. By the 1500s, up to four hundred thousand Native people lived in Florida.

Explorers and Settlers

In 1513, Spanish explorers sailed across the Atlantic Ocean. Juan Ponce de León led them. When he found Florida, he thought it was a

IN FLORIDA'S HISTORY

Europeans and Native Americans
Explorers to Florida came from Spain, France, and Britain. Some of them fought Native people. The explorers killed some Natives. They made others become slaves. Explorers from Europe also brought diseases. Many Native Americans got sick and died.

beautiful island. He claimed it for Spain and gave the land its name.

French and Spanish people began settling in Florida. In 1564, the French built Fort Caroline on the St. Johns River. Then, the Spanish built the city of St. Augustine. They drove out the French.

The British also tried to claim the land. France, Spain, and Britain fought for the area for many years.

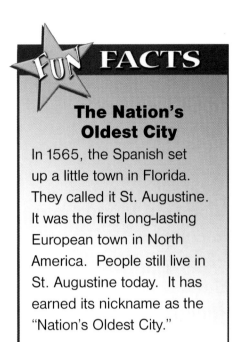
St. Mark's fort was built from 1672 to 1695 to guard the city of St. Augustine.

By 1600, Spain controlled it. In 1763, after a war in Europe, Spain gave Florida to Britain.

Two Floridas

Britain split Florida into two **colonies** — East Florida and West Florida. It did not keep these colonies for long.

Britain had other colonies in North America. Some of these colonies fought a war against Britain. This war was called the Revolutionary War. Most of the colonies won their freedom in 1783. They became the United States of America.

Florida still belonged to Britain. When Britain lost the war, however, Britain gave Florida back to Spain. British settlers left Florida. Spanish settlers arrived.

IN FLORIDA'S HISTORY

Andrew Jackson's War

In the early 1800s, when Florida belonged to Spain, U.S. general Andrew Jackson invaded Florida. Jackson almost caused a war with Spain. He also fought Natives there. In 1819, the U. S. paid Spain for the damage he had caused.

Escaped prisoners and runaway slaves moved in, too. Spain and the United States argued about Florida's border. In 1819, Spain agreed to give Florida to the United States.

The Territory of Florida

Florida became a U.S. **territory** in 1822. New settlers poured in. Many moved onto land where Native people lived. The Natives tried to drive the settlers away. The U.S. Army came to Florida. U.S. soldiers killed many Native people. They forced other Natives to move away. By 1858, only about two hundred Native Americans lived in Florida. They no longer had good land. Most of them hid in swamps.

Union and Reunion

Florida became the twenty-seventh state on March 3, 1845. Sixteen years later, the United States split into two nations. Florida and other southern states wanted to keep slavery. They formed the Confederate States of America. Northern states wanted to end slavery and keep the **Union** whole. The North and South fought the Civil War.

After the Union won the war, Florida and the other southern states rejoined the United States of America.

Famous People of Florida

Osceola

Born: About 1804, Alabama or Georgia

Died: January 30, 1838, Charleston, South Carolina

Osceola was a Native American and a leader of the Seminole people. In 1830, the U.S. government tried to force Native people to leave Florida. Osceola urged his people to stay. War broke out between the Seminoles and U.S. forces in 1835. Osceola fought fiercely for his people's land. In 1837, U.S. soldiers asked him to meet. He believed they wanted to discuss a truce, so he agreed. When he arrived for the meeting, the soldiers captured him and threw him in prison. Osceola died of disease a few months later. The stone over his grave says "Patriot and Warrior."

FACTS

Henry Flagler and the Florida East Coast Railway

Henry Flagler gave Florida a big boost. In the 1880s, he started to build the Florida East Coast Railway. Along the way, he started building hotels for **tourists**. Trains on his railroad carried oranges and other **produce** from Florida to markets in the north. The trains also brought tourists to Florida's beaches. Flagler's hotels gave the tourists places to stay. The state became known for its produce. It also became a popular vacation spot.

A Time of Growth

In the late 1800s, new businesses rose up in Florida. Cities and towns grew. People raised cattle.

Florida in the Civil War

The Civil War lasted from 1861 until 1865. Soldiers from Florida fought in the Confederate army. Florida also supplied food to the Confederates. Union forces captured cities on Florida's coast. The Confederates kept control inland. The Union won the Civil War.

They mined **phosphate**. Farmers drained swamps. Then, they grew oranges and other **citrus** fruits on the land. New hotels were built. A railroad was built, too. Trains carried fruits to markets in the north. They also brought tourists from colder states. By the early 1900s, people were also coming to Florida by car.

Disaster and War

Florida's economy was hurt in the late 1920s. Fruit flies damaged citrus crops.

Key West is a popular place to visit. It is in a chain of islands off the southern tip of Florida. Boating, diving, and other water sports draw many tourists to the area.

Hurricanes struck the state. In the 1930s, the **Great Depression** hit the whole country.

During World War II (1939–1945), U.S. soldiers trained in Florida. Military bases opened there. New airports and roads brought more tourists. Many people also decided to move to Florida and live there.

Florida in the News

In 2000, events in Florida affected the whole country. That year, the election for U.S. president was very close. Some votes in Florida were hard to read. Officials had to recheck and recount them. The country waited one month to see who its next president would be.

In July 1969, the *Apollo 11* spacecraft blasted off from the Kennedy Space Center at Cape Canaveral. The flight took people to the Moon for the first time ever.

Sometimes, Florida is in the news for its huge storms. Hurricanes often strike the state. These storms bring high winds and heavy rain. In 1992, Hurricane Andrew hit. It caused more damage than any storm in U.S. history. In 2004, four hurricanes hit the state in six weeks. They caused a lot of damage, too. Many people died in these fierce storms.

FUN FACTS

Into Space

In 1958, the first U.S. space satellite was launched from Cape Canaveral. Florida became a center for exploring space.

1513	Juan Ponce de León sails to the coast of Florida. He claims the land for Spain.
1565	The Spanish settle St. Augustine. It is the first long-lasting European settlement in North America.
1763	Spain gives Florida to Britain.
1783	Britain gives Florida to Spain.
1819	Spain gives Florida to the United States.
1835–1842	The U.S. government forces most Seminoles out of Florida.
1845	Florida becomes the twenty-seventh state.
1861–1865	The Civil War is fought.
1880s	Henry Flagler begins to build Florida East Coast Railway.
1920–1925	Florida becomes a popular place to buy land.
1958	The first U.S. satellite is launched from Cape Canaveral.
2000	Unclear votes in Florida delay the results of the U.S. presidential election.
2004	A series of strong hurricanes hits the state.

People

More than seventeen million people live in Florida. Its **population** keeps growing. Many **retired** people live in Florida. The average age of its residents is the highest in the nation.

Florida now has twice as many residents as it did in 1975. It has grown from the ninth-largest state to the fourth largest state!

People have come to Florida for many reasons. The first people were Native

Hispanics: In the 2000 U.S. Census, 16.8 percent of the people living in Florida called themselves Latino or Hispanic. Most of them or their relatives came from Spanish-speaking back-grounds. They may come from different racial backgrounds.

The People of Florida

Total Population 17,397,161

White
78%

Native American and Alaska Native
0.3%

Asian
1.7%

Other
5.4%

Black or African American
14.6%

Percentages are based on the 2000 Census.

14

This Seminole family lived in the Everglades in the 1970s. Here they are shown outside their home. They are displaying pottery they have made.

Americans. They may have come to find food.

Europeans came in the 1500s. The Spanish called the Native Americans "Seminoles." Europeans killed most Seminoles or drove them out. Many Natives moved away. Florida now has few Native Americans. Some live on reservations.

Escape from Slavery

Many African Americans came to Florida looking for freedom from slavery. They first arrived in the 1600s. Florida then belonged to Spain. They came from Virginia, Georgia, and other British colonies. By the mid-1800s, Florida was a U. S. state. About half the people there were black. Most of them were escaped slaves. Some hid in swamps. They stayed away from people who wanted them to go back to slavery again.

Famous People of Florida

James Weldon Johnson

Born: June 17, 1871, Jacksonville. Florida

Died: June 26, 1938, Wiscasset, Maine

James Weldon Johnson was the first African American to become a lawyer in Florida. He also taught at Fisk University in Nashville, Tennessee. This university was founded in 1866 to educate slaves who had just been freed. Johnson led the National Association for the Advancement of Colored People (NAACP) in the 1920s. A song he wrote with his brother, "Lift Ev'ry Voice and Sing," became known as the "Negro National Anthem."

After the Civil War, all of the slaves were freed. Many African Americans stayed in Florida.

Population Growth

In the late 1800s, farmers moved to Florida. By the early 1900s, it was a popular place to live. People came from northern states. They also came from other countries.

In 1959, Fidel Castro took over Cuba, an island country that is only 90 miles (145 km) from Florida. Some Cubans did not like the changes he made. They moved to Florida. Haiti is near Florida, too. Many Haitians moved to Florida as well. Miami is a city that is home to many people from Latin America and the Caribbean.

Today, all kinds of people live in Florida. Some come

to work or raise a family. Others come to retire where the weather is warmer.

Education and Religion

Florida had few public schools before the Civil War. After the war, a school system was created for the whole state. About sixty years ago, the state began giving money to the poorest schools. They wanted to be sure that every child could get a basic education. Florida has ten state universities now, too.

More than 80 percent of the people in Florida are Christians. Smaller numbers of people are Jews, Muslims, Hindus, and Buddhists.

People flock to Florida for fun in the sun, sand, and surf.

The Land

Florida is long and narrow. The only wide part is in the north, next to Georgia and Alabama. This part is called the "panhandle."

The rest of Florida is a **peninsula**. Water surrounds it on three sides. The Atlantic Ocean lies to the east and south. The Gulf of Mexico lies to the west. Sandy beaches line the coasts.

The state is mostly low and flat. Much of it is swamp. Huge areas of swamp are now national parks. The most famous park is the Everglades. It is in the southern part of the state.

Florida has no mountains. The panhandle has low hills. The highest point in the state is Britton Hill. This hill is only 345 feet (105 meters) high.

Many islands lie off Florida's coasts. The most famous islands are the Florida Keys. They stretch from the state's southern tip.

FUN FACTS

The Everglades

The Everglades is a huge national park. It takes up most of the southern tip of the state. Most of the park is a swamp with large areas of saw grass, pine trees, and mangrove trees. Hundreds of kinds of birds live there. Alligators, swamp animals, and fish live there, too. Millions of people visit the park every year. Now, about half of the wetlands have been drained so that people can use the land. Scientists are looking for ways to protect the land and the animals and plants that live there.

FLORIDA

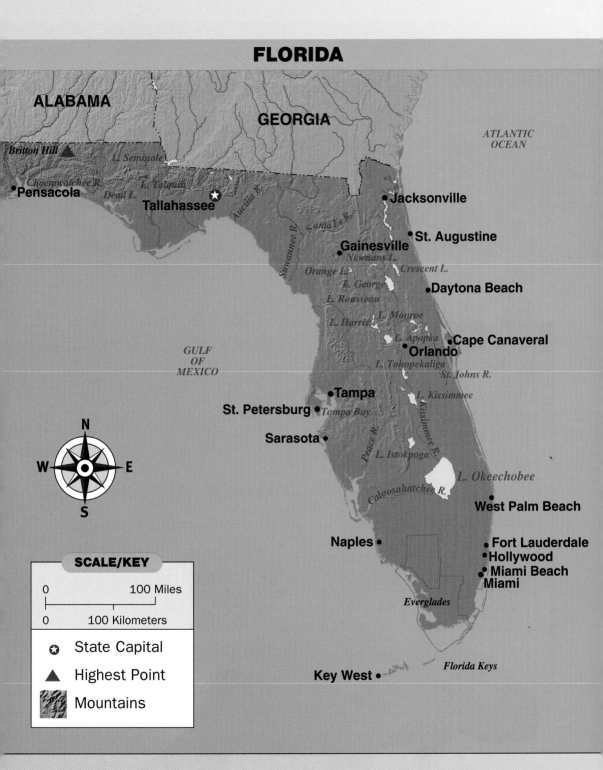

ALABAMA

GEORGIA

ATLANTIC OCEAN

Britton Hill

Choctawatchee R.

•Pensacola

L. Seminole

Dead L.

L. Talquin

Tallahassee

Aucilla R.

Suwannee R.

Santa Fe R.

•Jacksonville

•St. Augustine

Gainesville

Newnans L.

Orange L.

Crescent L.

L. George

•Daytona Beach

L. Rousseau

L. Harris

L. Monroe

•Orlando

L. Apopka

•Cape Canaveral

GULF OF MEXICO

L. Tohopekaliga

St. Johns R.

•Tampa

L. Kissimmee

St. Petersburg•

Tampa Bay

Sarasota•

Peace R.

Kissimmee R.

L. Istokpoga

L. Okeechobee

Caloosahatchee R.

West Palm Beach

Naples•

•Fort Lauderdale

•Hollywood

•Miami Beach

Miami

Everglades

Key West •

Florida Keys

N
W E
S

SCALE/KEY

0	100 Miles
0	100 Kilometers

⊗ State Capital

▲ Highest Point

▨ Mountains

Waterways

Thousands of lakes dot the state's middle part. Lake Okeechobee is one of the largest lakes in the nation. It is very shallow, however. Its deepest point is only 9 feet (2.75 m)!

Major Rivers

St. Johns River
285 miles (459km) long

Suwannee River
250 miles (402 km) long

Choctawhatchee River
140 miles (225 km) long

The longest river is the St. Johns River. The Suwannee River is smaller, but it is more famous. The state song, "Swanee River," is named after it.

FUN FACTS

Florida's Manatees

One of the most interesting animals in Florida is the manatee. Manatees live in rivers and coastal waters. Manatees are huge. They look a little like walruses, but they are not related to walruses. They are related to elephants. It is against the law to harm a manatee.

Warm Weather, Big Storms

Florida has warm weather year-round. Summer days are hot and humid. Winters are mild.

Florida usually gets at least one hurricane a year in the late summer and the fall.

Plants and Animals

Forests cover parts of the state. Pines and many other kinds of trees grow there. Florida is known for its **mangrove**, palm, and magnolia trees.

More than four hundred kinds of birds live in Florida. The state has many pelicans and herons. Eagles nest there, too. Flamingos and ospreys live along the coast.

The state also has many reptiles. Alligators snooze in the warm waters. Snakes slither through swamps and forests. Some snakes in Florida are poisonous. These snakes include coral snakes and rattlesnakes.

Florida has more kinds of fish than any other place in the world. It has big bass in its lakes. Huge fish, such as tarpon and sailfish, swim in the ocean.

As more people move to Florida, its largest animals are losing their homes. Laws now protect some animals. These laws protect Florida panthers, black bears, and Key deer.

Pink flamingos live in Florida's subtropical climate.

Economy

Tourism creates many jobs in Florida. Millions of tourists visit the state every year. They stay in hotels. They eat in restaurants. They visit theme parks, such as Walt Disney World and Universal Studios. Many people work in these places. Other workers help people who live in the state. Some are doctors and lawyers. Others are bankers, teachers, and real estate agents.

These oranges are ripe for picking at an orange grove in Florida.

Fishing

Many people have jobs catching fish. Some people catch shrimp. Others catch catfish, tuna, and grouper.

Farming and Other Jobs

Farming also provides jobs. Oranges are Florida's top crop. Grapefruit and other citrus fruits are important, too. Tomatoes are the next-biggest crop.

Farmers grow many kinds of fruits and vegetables in the mild weather. They also raise cattle and chickens.

Florida has a large mining industry. Phosphate and other minerals are found here. The state also has many **high-tech** companies. They create computer software and other high-tech products.

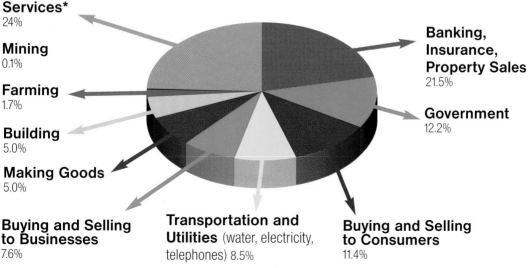

How Money Is Made in Florida

Services*
24%

Mining
0.1%

Farming
1.7%

Building
5.0%

Making Goods
5.0%

Banking, Insurance, Property Sales
21.5%

Government
12.2%

Buying and Selling to Businesses
7.6%

Transportation and Utilities (water, electricity, telephones) 8.5%

Buying and Selling to Consumers
11.4%

* Services include jobs in hotels, restaurants, auto repair, medicine, teaching, and entertainment.

23

Government

Tallahassee is Florida's capital city. The state's leaders work there. Florida's government has three parts, or branches. They are the executive, legislative, and judicial branches.

GREAT SEAL OF THE STATE OF FLORIDA
IN GOD WE TRUST

Executive Branch

The governor heads the executive branch. This branch makes sure that state laws are carried out. The lieutenant governor helps the governor. Six other officials belong to the governor's **cabinet**, or team.

The old Florida state capitol building is now a state museum. Behind it is the new capitol, which was completed in 1977.

The Florida legislature meets for sixty days each year. The House and the Senate must agree on each bill before it becomes a law.

Legislative Branch

The legislative branch makes state laws. The legislature has two bodies. It has a Senate and a House of Representatives. The Senate and the House work together.

Judicial Branch

Judges and courts make up the judicial branch. Judges **interpret** the state's laws, especially when someone is **accused of** a crime.

County Governments

Florida is divided into sixty-seven counties. Each county has its own government and its own rules.

FLORIDA'S STATE GOVERNMENT

Executive		Legislative		Judicial	
Office	**Length of Term**	**Body**	**Length of Term**	**Court**	**Length of Term**
Governor	4 years	Senate (40 members)	4 years	Supreme (7 justices)	6 years
Lieutenant Governor	4 years	House of Representatives		Appeals	6 years
		(120 members)	2 years		

Things to See and Do

Disney World in Orlando is the most popular tourist spot in the United States! More than fifteen million people visit it each year. Disney World has many areas. Epcot Center has a huge dome with a science museum inside it. At Disney-MGM Studios, visitors see how movies are made. Universal Studios, Sea World, and other theme parks are also in Orlando.

Florida has beaches on both coasts. Most of them have soft, white sand. In winter,

FUN FACTS

Spaceship Earth

Epcot Center includes a building called Spaceship Earth. The building is round, like a golf ball. And what a big ball it is — seventeen stories high! It can be seen from miles away. Visitors to Epcot can go inside, walk around, and watch shows about life on Earth over thousands of years.

Mary McLeod Bethune

Born: July 10, 1875, Mayesville, South Carolina

Died: May 18, 1955, Daytona Beach, Florida

Mary Bethune McLeod was African American. Her parents had been slaves. After she grew up, Mary started a school for black girls in Daytona Beach. Twenty years later, that school became the first college in the United States ever started by a black woman. Mary became a famous teacher and an adviser to five U.S. presidents. She often spoke in favor of equal rights for black people. She also fought for good jobs for black people, especially black women.

people from the north flock to these beaches.

National Parks

Many kinds of animals live in the Everglades. Dry Tortugas National Park is known for its sea turtles and coral reef. Biscayne National Park has a beautiful coral reef and a mangrove forest.

Alligators live in the Everglades.

Sports

Florida has professional sports teams. Football fans watch the Miami Dolphins and Tampa Bay Buccaneers. Basketball fans cheer for the Miami Heat and the Orlando Magic. The Florida Marlins and the Tampa Bay Devil Rays play baseball there. Hockey fans love the Florida Panthers and the Tampa Bay Lightning.

In spring, many baseball teams practice in Florida. They play spring training games as part of their practice. Florida also has many college sports teams.

Latin American Culture

People who go to Miami often visit Little Havana. This neighborhood is named after Havana, Cuba. People from all over the United States and Latin America live in Little Havana. They speak Spanish and play Latin music. **Vendors** sell food on the streets. A trip to Little Havana

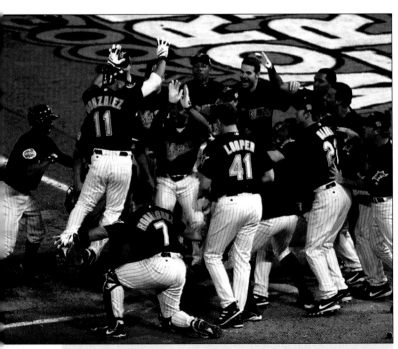

The Florida Marlins celebrate a big win in the 2003 World Series.

feels like a visit to another country.

Circus Museum

The Ringling Museum of the Circus is in Sarasota. Here, visitors can learn all about circus history. They can even see how one circus became "The Greatest Show on Earth."

These trays are on display in Miami's Little Havana. They are filled with magnets that look like fresh fruit.

Famous People of Florida

Jacqueline Cochran

Born: About 1910, Pensacola, Florida

Died: August 9, 1980, Indio, California

At a time when few women flew airplanes, Jacqueline Cochran was setting records. In the late 1930s and early 1940s, she learned to fly and started racing. She was the first woman to break the speed of sound. Her plane traveled at 625.5 miles (1,006 km) per hour. She was the first woman to make a "blind" landing. She was also the first woman to fly a warplane across the Atlantic Ocean. By 1961, she held more speed records than any other pilot in the world.

★ ★

accused of — blamed for

cabinet — a team of people who help a political leader make decisions

citrus — a group of fruits that includes oranges, grapefruits, tangerines, limes, and lemons

colonies — groups of people living in a new land but keeping ties with the place they came from

Great Depression — a time, in the 1930s, when many people and businesses lost money

high-tech — having to do with computers

interpret — to explain the meaning of something

mangrove — a tropical tree that sends out many roots

peninsula — a piece of land that is nearly surrounded by water

phosphate — a material used in fertilizers

population — the number of people who live in a place, such as a city, town, or state

produce — fresh fruits and vegetables

retired — no longer working at a job

territory — an area that belongs to a country

tourists — people who travel for pleasure

Union — the United States of America

vendors — people who sell goods, such as food, toys, or jewelry

Books

Everglades. Jean Craighead George (HarperCollins)

Florida A to Z. Susan Ryan (Pineapple Press)

Hurricane! The Rage of Hurricane Andrew. True Adventure (series). Patricia Lantier-Sampon (Gareth Stevens)

The Manatees of Florida. Animals of the World (series). Bill Lund (Bridgestone)

Panther: Shadow of the Swamp. Jonathan London (Candlewick)

The Seminole. Native Americans (series). Richard M. Gaines (Checkerboard Library)

Web Sites

Florida Kids' Page
dhr.dos.state.fl.us/kids/

Kennedy Space Center
www.kennedyspacecenter.com/launches/index.asp

Museum of Florida History
dhr.dos.state.fl.us/museum/

Seminole Indians
www.mnsu.edu/emuseum/cultural/northamerica/
seminole.html

INDEX

★ ★